Whore's Lake

Whore's Lake

Ruth Jackson

To order additional copies of this book, contact:
Xlibris Corporation
1-888-795-4274
www.Xlibris.com
Orders@Xlibris.com
69886

Chapter 1

S OMEWHERE IN THE world there is a lake, a deep
black lake with large stumps sticking up out of the
water. It is scary. When I was a kid, I was afraid of this
lake, and no one would get into it because of what the
people would say.

They say that so many women would be thrown into
it and they died. They were all black women who were
thrown into the lake by white men. All my life I heard this
story. This lake ran down each side of a road. The only
way we could leave was to travel on it. When it would
rain, the lake would overflow and flood the road.

It was very spooky and dark; you saw fish and
everything else in it. I heard that the black women were
prostitutes. We were told so many women were put in to
the lake; that's why it's called Whore's Lake.

As a child, I was told that white men would kill black women to keep them from telling anyone else about what happened. At this time, most blacks worked on farms and plantations. All the lakes around there would be used to catch fish for food, but not this one.

Where we lived, there were about two thousand blacks and five hundred whites. This little town was so small; they had only one sheriff or policeman. He was so mean. He was so tall and heavy, he would waddle when he walked. I would call him Good, Rocking Daddy. At this time, I was a young girl, and we were told to not look at white men or talk to them because we were told tall tales about the police.

Now he is an older man, but when he was a young man long ago, there were lots of beautiful young black women around here.

He would get them to work for his wife, and no one would ever see them again. All were not street women or prostitutes. At that time, black people could not accuse a white man or a policeman, no way. The black man would move away from there.

The black men knew if they said anything, they would have to move because they knew that they and their families would be in trouble. They say that these black girls would come to town to shop on Saturday, and the sheriff would stop them to asked, "Whose child are you?" or "Whose plantation are you living on?" Then he would say, "I know him."

He is a fine man; most folks call him Big John—I guess that was his name. There was a family, they said, that lived at one time about two miles from town and worked on a plantation called the Jeffersons. The husband, William, and his wife, Louis, had six children—the oldest son, Frank; a second son, Jessie; the oldest girl, Lillie; a second girl, Kate; the youngest son, James; and a baby girl, Jeanie.

Kate was sixteen when this happened. She was tall, had brown hair and brown eyes—a beauty, they say. When she walked into a room, heads turned.

And so on her sixteenth birthday, Kate was so excited and happy just to go to town. Back then, children did not go to town every week. Their parents went to town; kids stayed home. Kate was the most beautiful one of all; she was small with light brown skin and long thick brown hair.

So on her sixteenth birthday, she went to town with some of her friends and some of her neighbors that lived down the road from her. They were the Roberts; their daughter was Lillie Roberts. She was also sixteen years old. They got in the car with some boys and went to town, but Kate did not come back.

When they first came over to talk to Kate's father about letting her go, he said, "No, I don't think so."

But Kate's mom said, "William, let the child go out with them. Lizzie is a nice girl, and the young boys, we know them too."

So Kate's dad said, "Okay. But you all be back before dark."

It was summer. It did not get dark until about 9:00 p.m. Okay, so they took off in an old car, which belonged to one of the boys' dads. The one driving was Rob Hill, and the other was Bill Ross. Rob liked Kate, and Bill liked Lizzie. So they got to Drew that evening, and Lizzie and Kate got out of the car, just playing and talking to each other.

Big John walked up. He looked at Kate and said, "What's your name, whose gal are you?"

Kate smiled and said, "Mr. John, I am Kate Jefferies. We live on the West Plantation."

Big John said, "Oh yes, I know who you are now." So they went to the café, Kate and her friends, and Big John went on down the street. Kate and her friends danced, ate, and talked for about three hours.

Then Rob said, "We should go because you know what your dad said. You got to be home before dark." This was on a weekday, a Thursday. So they got in the car to go home. Lizzie and Bill were kissing in back of the car, and Rob pulled out to go home.

Big John drove up behind them and told them to get out of the car, and he put them in a police car and told them that Rob was not old enough to drive and that they were doing the nasty in back of the car. They tried to tell him the truth, but he told them, "Just shut up. I'm going to tell your dad in the morning. I will ride out there." And he split them up. He put Rob and Bill in a cell together and Lizzie and Kate each by themselves. Then later he let all of them go but Kate. And they asked him, "Is Kate still there?"

"No, I let her go too. I don't know where she went."

Then Big John told them to go home, and they left crying because they could not find Kate. All the way home, they could not talk to each other for crying by it, being after dark. Kate's dad was in the window, looking out for them. When they drove up, he looked and said, "I don't see her."

He said to his wife, "I see the other three kids." In the meantime, Big John went into Kate's cell and raped her and beat her then took her to the lake. Then he raped and beat her until she died. He left her on the lake with no clothes on her body.

Then he pissed on her body and went back to town as if nothing had happened at all.

Big John was a madman. Kate's mom and dad asked, "What happened? Where is Kate?" They were so upset they could not think. They were crying; everyone was crying, including her other sisters and brothers.

So her dad says, "Louis, honey, let's go into town to ask the sheriff. Maybe Kate is in town with no way home. That's right, we will go look for her. I got to find Kate."

So they got in the car and went by Rod Hill's home to tell his father and mother. So they left the boys, and the four parents went into Drew to find Big John. He was at the jail, just sitting there looking crazy. In the meantime he had washed up and changed clothes. So they saw him when they got to town.

They went in and asked him, "Sheriff, did you let Kate go with the other kids?" He got up. "Well, sure I did, William, I let all of them go. I would not have kept her. They were doing the nasty in the car. Did they tell you that that's why I stopped them? I just wanted to scare them, I let all of them go home. You should ask that boy who was hanging all over her."

And Rob's dad said, "That's my boy, and he is not like that, Sheriff, and he would not do anything to Kate. I know he would not."

So the sheriff said, "I bet she is already at home waiting for you. You all go home, you will find her." So they drove all around town, looking for Kate. Her mother was so hurt, she could not talk in the car. She just said, "Please, William, find Kate, find my baby." All that night they could not sleep. The neighbors all came over to wait with them, but Kate did not come home. William and Louis knew that the sheriff had done something to their child, but they could not prove it. They could not do anything either because he was white and they were black, and he was the sheriff.

After about two days, two men were walking, and they saw a naked black girl dead. Before it became known as Whore's Lake, people did fish in it, and the water was clear.

Chapter 2

AFTER THIS, MORE murders began to happen in Drew. There were whorehouses and prostitutes. And there was a prostitute named Sugar Foot who walked the street. She was half crazy. She was found about three months after Kate, naked and her body pissed on after she was dead. She also was black. She was the second woman.

The people were getting worried about what was going on, and they would not let their young daughters go out by themselves. The sheriff was all down in the woods, trying to get some clues, but the whole time, he was the one who was killing these women.

Then the sheriff would walk the streets looking like a mad dog, looking for someone to kill. He was so upset with those black girls, he began beating his wife. Then talk was going on in Drew about the law. Some of them were moving from Mississippi because of the sheriff. No matter what the sheriff did to black girls, nothing would be done anyway. So one day, all the fathers went to work in the fields, and the young kids were home with one of the young girls, and a white man came to the door and tried to get in.

He was dressed as an old man, but it was the sheriff. He pulled out a dollar, then he pulled opened the door and just went in and raped a ten-year-old girl. And there were two other kids. They were watching him. Then he got back in his car and rode away. When he left, the girl ran across the field, crying and bleeding because he had beaten her.

Then her mother and father ran to her, screaming, "What happened to you?" She said, "Daddy, it was an old white man in a police car." The daddy asked Susan, "Was it the sheriff in the car?"

She said, "No, it was another man, Daddy."

So they took Susan to a doctor. Sure enough, she was raped, but by who? They could not ask the sheriff if he was in their house. The young girl's life was messed up, and the news spread all over the county. Most black folks were so afraid to leave their home. Big John, the sheriff, was drinking so much.

Most of the blacks started going to the nearby town just to get away from Big John.

And when he found out that there was no one coming to his town on Saturday nights, he started to go to the next town and search for a girl. So he went to this bar in the next town and found a party. Then he just sat outside in his car, drinking and watching the girls. But Kate's father would not let him get away with killing his child.

William Jefferies buried his daughter. Then he went to the man whose plantation he stayed on, Mr. Colman, and told him what had happened to his family and the sheriff in town. "He was white also," William said. "Mr. Colman, I don't have no one to help me with problems. I am afraid to come to you because I don't know who to trust now."

Mr. Colman told William, "I will help you, I like Kate. You and your family are nice people, I will help you." So Mr. Colman went to town to talk to the mayor in Drew about Big John.

The mayor was furious with Big John. The mayor was Mr. Gains. He said, "This is a mess. I don't need this at a time of election, all these black people leaving town because of a white sheriff. We need the colored folks to stay. Talk will get out about our town. What will people think? Let's talk to this man for God's sake."

So they went to the jail to see Big John. He was sitting at the window, just looking at them. The mayor heavy, and he was upset with Big John. So they went in, and Big John jumped up. "Look, I had nothing to do with that little tramp. Don't come here to put me in that. Mayor, now I don't know what Colman has told you. Them colored people live on his land, they work for him."

The mayor said, "Cool down, John. I just want to talk to you about what's going on around here, that's all."

Mr. Colman said, "I believe William because he has never lied to me. This man and his family are good colored folks."

Big John began throwing things around the room, saying, "You believe a black boy over me. Is that what you are saying, Colman?" Then the mayor got sick. He was sweating, and he was trying to stop them from fighting. So Mr. Colman said, "Leave that family alone, they work for me. And I am going to expose you so they can take that badge from you." They left Big John screaming at them. The mayor was so afraid of Big John. When he got outside of the jail, he said, "Big John, you are fired. You are no longer the sheriff no more, Big John. You are through being sheriff."

Both Mr. Colman and the mayor went home. Big John went home to his wife. He was no longer sheriff; everyone was so happy. But the killings kept on happening. Bodies keep being left on Whore's Lake. No one knew who did it. So the sheriff's wife asked him, "Why was you fired? Tell me. What are the people saying about you, John? I am your wife, I don't want to be the last person to know what's going on around here. People will talk, and I can't deal with a lot of problems. John, what will I tell our kids and my family? You know how that is."

He just looked at her and walked away, and then he went for a ride to the black part of the town. He was looking for a street woman, but he could not find one. Then he went to the next town, which was Clarksdale, about eighty miles from Drew, and he searched around town for someone.

The sheriff saw two young black girls walking down the road from the store in town. But these were church girls, Loris and Mary Ives—one was twelve years old, and the other was thirteen years old. Their father was a Baptist preacher, and their mother was a churchwoman. And they went to school in Clarksville, They had a very nice family and lived at the back of the town.

It was a Thursday night. The sheriff drove by them in his car then backed up to where they were walking. And he said, "Hi, girls, where you going?"

They said, "Home, Sheriff." He was still in the sheriff's car. So he smiled and said, "I will drop you off. Get in." So they got in the car, and he took them to a wooded place where he beat and raped them both, Then he killed them and removed their clothing and threw them all around.

Chapter 3

THESE GIRLS WERE beaten so bad, so he took them to Whore's Lake. Then he pissed on their bodies and laid them out on the side of the lake then walked and cried. When he finished, he broke down and cried, but went and did the same crime again.

So Big John went home this night, but this night wasn't like the other nights.

Neither of these girls were like the others; they were so young and innocent. This was real bad. Their mother was looking for them because they did not come back home from the store. So she sent their older brother James to look for them. He went to the store, and the store manager said, "They were here about an hour ago. Yes, they was in the store, but they left after they got what they wanted to buy. But I don't know where they went from here." So James went home and told his mother, then she sent two of her sons to the church to tell their father to come and hurry home now.

Then the whole church came to their home and prayed for them and cried. The mother was so upset over this. They had ten children, six girls and four boys. This was so horrible; no one in that part of town slept that night.

Everyone was awake. The mother was screaming and calling her two daughters, "Loris, Mary Ives, where are you? Please come home, come back home, my children." You could hear her for miles, screaming. Her husband and some of the deacons were riding around in cars, looking for the kids.

They looked everywhere but could not find them. So they stayed up all night, hoping for them to come home.

John went in his car and came to the back of his house, took off his clothes outside, and burned them up, Then he went in the garage and put on other clothing. Then he just stayed outside, cleaning out his car and washing up.

John's wife came out the back door to speak to him. "John, what are you doing out there?" she said to him. "I thought you was fired, John."

He said to her, "I am."

"Why then are you in that car?"

He said, "I am just cleaning it up before I give it back. They are not going to get a new sheriff anyway soon, not on this salary. No, no, they will beg me to go back to them for this sick job. Don't nobody want this sick job for this little money. Yes, you will see, just wait. They will beg me back."

Then his wife asked him, "John, why did you change, what happened to you?"

He said, "I had to break up a fight tonight. We had some trouble in town. You know we don't have law here now, someone has to show up. The mayor is not going to lift one finger. But he thinks he is the man."

*   *   *

But this was a night that the James family would never forget. Back at their home, the pain was so bad. So they went to town to the police station in Clarksville to talk to the sheriff. This sheriff was Ben Sheridan; he was a nice sheriff.

He came over to the James's house and said, "I am so sorry, Rev. James. I will get on the phone and call all the sheriff offices around here and try to find your children." And his wife came over to confront them, and she brought cookies pops because this would be a long night.

Early the next morning, the sheriff in Clarksville came over to talk to Rev. James and his wife. He told them that he had gotten in touch with other police departments in that county and said, "If I hear anything, I will let you know right away."

Then the sheriff added, "You know, Reverend, a few months back, I heard about a young colored girl in Drew come up missing, and I wish I could remember their last name, but I can't. But I will try and find out her name for you."

Rev. James said, "Thank you, Sheriff, for whatever you do to help my family."

So he left, but the girls did not come home anymore. And this family was looking everywhere all night for these two girls. Two days later, a man and his dogs were hunting and found their naked bodies lying by the water, and it was the way that Big John had laid them out.

The police came from all over to see the girls, and news spread about the crime. The sheriff of Clarksville came to the house for Rev. James, but they were all at the church praying. He called him and said, "Rev. James, I got some bad news."

And the Reverend James said, "Please just tell me, Sheriff."

And the sheriff said, "We found them, but they are dead."

And the Reverend James said, "Oh my god, oh my god, no, no!" And his wife came and hugged him, and they all came out of the church crying, weeping for them. "Now who did this to my children? Who would do such a thing as this?" the mother said. "My children did not do anything to anybody. Why, why?"

And the sheriff said, "I am so sorry." And he left with some other men to go to the coroner to see why they had died or how they were killed. The family got into their cars to go to the funeral home to see their dead children.

This was a time to mourn, but back in Drew where Big John lived, all hell had broken loose for him. Two policemen went to see the mayor in Drew and told him about the two young colored girls and what the other sheriff from Clarksville had said to ask him about—Big John and the murders. So they took the mayor to John's home. And John's wife was in the kitchen when they came, and Big John was sitting in the living room. They knocked on the door of his house, but Big John just sat there like he did not hear them at all, and they just kept knocking.

Chapter 4

THEN HIS WIFE came out of the kitchen. Her name was Ana. She said, "John, why don't you open the door and see who's there?"

He told her, "You can open it if you want to."

She opened the door, saying, "Come in, Mayor."

The policemen said, "We came to ask your husband some questions."

The mayor said, "I would like to speak to him alone."

But his wife Ana said, "No, I want to stay, mayor."

Then John said, "Well then, let her stay."

One of the policemen said, "John, where were you on Thursday night about eight or nine in the evening?"

John said to them, "I was home with my wife."

The mayor said to him, "Your wife. Well, I hope that she can speak to the sheriff of Clarksville about those two young colored girls."

And his wife said, "Oh my god, what two girls?"

One of the policemen said, "Ms. Ana, there have been least five colored girls killed in the last year. And now two young girls that belong to a Baptist minister in Clarksville was killed Thursday night and found naked on a lake in the woods north from here."

She said, "Why would you suspect my husband with colored girls?"

The policemen said, "Because we were told he might know something about the killings."

Ana asked the policemen, "Can I ask you something? Was those girls raped?"

They said, "Yes, all of them was raped, murdered, stripped of clothing, and pissed on. Their bodies laid out on the road beside of the lake."

Ana ran out of the back door and threw up in the yard. Then she just sat outside. The mayor came out, asked, "Ana, are you all right? Ana, what's wrong?" She just sat, crying and shaking her head. "No, no."

John said, "They not nothing but some cheap little whores. So what's the big deal? So what?"

The mayor said, "John, did you do that to the colored girls?"

John said, "No, who said I did? And if I did, no one can prove it. There has never been in the history of man a white man arrested for killing a black whore. You all know that if my forefathers knew this, they would turn over in their graves. You are coming to my house to ask me about this shit. Go to hell, Mayor, and both you police, just go to hell. I got friends, and, mayor, you are going to be in big trouble, nigger lovers. That's all nigger lovers." The mayor, who was very fat, started sweating profusely.

"John, you won't get away with this. I told you before. When that other girl, that Jefferies girl, was killed, that's why I fired you from being sheriff. Now you did this in my town!" The mayor was shouting and screaming at Big John. He had to sit down on the couch, then the two policemen tried to stop John from cursing at the mayor.

Ana ran into the house, screaming, "Mayor, did I hear you say that there was another girl? Did I hear that's why my husband lost his job? And you know what means for us all, so stay in your home."

John said, "Don't talk to anyone about this."

But Ana was screaming at John, "Oh no, I won't keep quiet for you anymore, John. I will not help you cover this up, not this time, John!"

The police had left. But in the meantime, Rev. James and his family and the church members started to get themselves ready to bury their children. Then they were all in the church crying, and the reverend was standing over the dead children, looking at them, crying.

Then suddenly, there was a loud knock on the door. It was the sheriff; he opened the door and just stood there. The sheriff was crying, and he had his hands over his eyes. "I did not do this, Rev. James, I did not. Someone is trying to put this on me. I would never do anything like this. Please believe me."

But the reverend's wife stood up and said, "Sheriff Mr. John, whoever killed my children, it is not up to us now, it's up to God if you did or not. Mr. John, it won't bring back my children. So we are not angry with you. God will punish whoever did this horrible thing." And she sat back down, and her husband was standing, looking at the sheriff. And Big John said, "Rev. James, will you please pray for me?

"Yes, Mr. John, I will." Then Big John left, still crying, and the Reverend James started to pray for a man that he believed killed his own two children. "How can I, Lord? But give me the strength, he is a lost soul. Help this man."

The reverend's oldest son, James Jr, could not shake loose what had happened to his little sisters.

Chapter 5

T HIS THING WAS getting to him. So his mother tried to talk to him after the funeral was over. That day in the kitchen at dinner, he was quiet and withdrawn from everyone. His mother said, "Son, please let it go, let God handle this. Nothing we do will bring them home again. I know you are hurt, we all are. Don't mess up your life. We are in Mississippi. The white man's world. I don't want you to hate Mr. John."

Her son said, "But, Mom, I do hate with a passion to kill him."

She said, "Oh no, my son. Don't feel like this."

Then she called her husband. "James, come in here. Talk to your son. I don't want to hear this at this time. I can't handle this now. Please, James, talk to him now."

So her husband, James, walking in to the kitchen, said, "What's going on, dear? We have guests here."

Then she told him, "Our son is talking crazy, talk to him. I can't, not now."

The father said, "James, my son, I am a pastor and a man of God. I want to kill the man that did this. But, son, I know I can't. I want to if I knew for sure. I can't, but I would like to. That's human nature.

"But we can't kill someone just because we want to or because we don't like someone. Please get this out of your mind. Your mom and I have enough to worry about now, we don't want to start worrying about you now. You have been a good kid.

"We never had any trouble out of you, son. It hurts me to think about my kids, what they went through before their death. But, son, no one can hurt them now. This is a cruel world."

But James started drinking heavily and running around with some other bad kids. It seemed like this thing that happened had shaken him to the core. He hated all white people from then on, and this worried his parents.

His father preached not to hate anyone. So after a while, things began to settle. And there were no murders for a while, and they went back to their lives. But they never forgot the four kids that were murdered.

They moved on, and Big John's wife Ana left him. She went to stay with her mother, and she took their kids. And

Big John stayed in the house by himself. About six months had passed since the two sisters were murdered.

It was Thanksgiving, and Big John was so lonely, and he began to drink and drink. He had his home so messed up with beer bottles. And they had gotten another sheriff in Drew named Mr. Flemming, and he was much better than Big John.

Big John started crying for his wife. He said, "This is a time for my family, my wife and kids." So he got into his car and went over to his wife's mother's house to see them.

He was so drunk, nasty, dirty, and smelly that his wife was embarrassed to see him. They were having dinner and had guests over at her mother's house. He rang the doorbell, crying. He said, "Ana, can I come in?" Her mother opened the door. He did not even speak to her mother; he just walked in. "Ana, I love you. Ana, please come back home. I am so lonely, you have no idea."

Raising her voice, Ana said, "John, John, stop it now. We are about to serve dinner. Speak to your kids, John. You have not seen them for a while. And why did you come into my mother's house drunk and not speak to her?

"John, look at yourself. What's going on in your head?"

He said, "I don't know, I just want you back to help me. I need you to help me, Ana."

"No," she said in a loud voice. "No more, John. I can't go back."

He never shouted at his two sons, Billie and Joe. Billie was seven, and Joe was ten. He also had one girl. Her name was Peggy; she was eight. They were afraid of him when he was drunk.

So he started to cry then. He got mad and said in a loud voice, "I know you have a man here, Ana. That's why you are doing this to me. But I am going to fix you for this, and you won't take my family from me. I love you, Ana."

Then he left the home of her mother, speeding away fast. The family of Ana watched him from her windows. They could not believe how he carried on. Then on his way back to his house, he stopped at a bar and kept on drinking. John left there and went to another club for coloreds, and he sat outside drinking. And when the club was closed, he waited for a chance to talk to someone. But they were all with someone else. John just sat outside, drinking from a bottle and talking to himself.

So when the club was closed about 2:00 a.m., John was still waiting, and after everyone had left, only the club owner and one of the barmaids were left. So he asked for one of them to give him a beer.

But they told him that they were closed for the night, and he went on. But he hid in the brush beside the club. When the barmaid got paid and tried to go to her car, he grabbed her. She was a twenty-six-year-old woman named Pearl Black from Lealin, Mississippi. She was married and had one child, a girl named Bettie, and a husband named Sam Black.

He took her in his car. This happened on a Thursday night—Thanksgiving.

Her husband was waiting for her at home. He had fixed a big dinner for her, but she had to work late, and he fell asleep.

John knocked her down to the ground and beat her in the head and face till she passed out in his car. Big John was still drinking and talking to himself about his wife, Ana, and how he was going to fix everybody in that town. He said, "I will show them just who to mess with. Yes, I am going to show them." He was talking about the mayor, his wife, and the new sheriff, Mr. Flemming.

He was very quiet as he drove to Whore's Lake that night. Pearl Black lay in his car, bleeding. He took her to the woods by the lake and stripped her and beat her some more then pissed on her naked body. He tried to rape her, but he was so drunk he could barely stand up. John began cursing and fell into the lake. Then Pearl started to crawl away with no clothing on. She tried to get away from him. John finally got out of the lake and tried to find her, but he was so drunk and could not think right. So he called to her, "Barmaid, where are you? Hey, you, come back. I won't hurt you, I swear."

But she lay still in the mud and weeds by the lake's bank, looking at him. John got in his car and left, almost killing himself. He went to his house and shut the door.

Pearl, she was hurt pretty bad. She washed off the blood that was on her face. She got up, trying to walk. She saw a light from a distance. She did not live around there; she lived about thirty miles from Drew. But she walked to a house that sat out in a field. This house had a black family that lived there.

And she came to the door, naked, at three in the morning. The weather was cold. She was bleeding all over. The man at the house did not want to open the door for her.

Pearl kept on knocking, and he said, "Who is it? Who is it?"

She could barely stand up, and she said, "Pearl. Please let me in. I am hurt bad."

That man was Marven Jones. His wife, Pat, came and opened the door. Pat Jones could not believe her eyes. There stood a naked woman, crying and bleeding. Pat said, "Who are you, and what happened to you?" Her husband, Marvin, jumped up from the bed and said, "Oh my god!"

And Pat put a sheet over Pearl's body. Then Pearl fell on a chair and just sat down, crying.

Marvin started to get the fire going. They slept in their front room, and Pat got some water and gave it to Pearl to wash her face. Pearl said thank you. Pearl said, "I am

Pearl Black. I live in Lealin, I work at the club there. And I am married and have a child. I have been attacked by the man who killed all those colored girls by that lake. And I think he was trying to kill me, but he smelled like a liquor bar. He fell into the lake, and when he was trying to get out, I crawled away. He beat me and pissed on me." Then she started to cry again. Pat just hugged her and said, "I am so sorry for you. I can't believe this, do you know this man?" Pat asked her.

Pearl said, "No, but he was white. I saw him when he came in the club and asked for a beer. When we were closing, he then left—or so I thought."

So Marvin got the fire going in the stove. The house was warm. Pat gave Pearl some of her clothes to put on. Pat and Marvin did not have a car, but they knew the Jefferies. This was cake family. They lived down the road. So Marvin said to Pat, "I am going down to Mr. Jefferies' house so she can get home to her family."

Pat said, "Okay, go ahead, Marvin, but watch out for that killer." Marvin went to Mr. Jefferies, knocking on the door at four in the morning, and told him about what had happened to Pearl. They were terrified by this man, of how he could keep doing this to colored women.

Nothing was being done at all to him. "I can't believe this. He killed my little girls, I know he did. This is not right," said Mr. Jefferies.

Mr. Jefferies and his wife went back with Marvin to his house, and they all got in to his old car and went to

Lealin, Mississippi, to take Pearl home. She cried all the way there.

Pearl's husband was standing out in front of their home, looking for her. He had been to her office and got the car and brought it home. Sam talked to the sheriff in Lealin, Mississippi. But they did not have a clue of what had happened to his wife.

When the old car drove up and Pearl crawled out all beaten up, he just came and hugged his wife, asking, "What happened to you? What happened?"

She said, "The sheriff tried to kill me. He did this to me, he did this when I came out. He hit me, knocking me to the ground. I could not fight him, but I got away."

Her husband went crazy. "I will kill him! I don't care if he is the sheriff or if he is white. I don't care!"

Then Mr. Jefferies said, "Mr. Black, listen to me, I been through this. The same man killed our little girl Kate, she was sixteen years old. This man is the devil himself. He is not a sheriff no more. But he keeps on killing young colored girls. We got to stop him some way."

Marvin said, "But what can we do?"

Mr. Jefferies said, "I know someone we can talk to. Let's wait until dawn, and then we will talk to your sheriff here in Lealin, first of all. We got to do something."

So they just sat and talk and drank coffee, and Marvin spoke to Sam Black, trying to cool him down. Pearl had to lie down. Girl was asleep. Never knew anything. It was about nine in the morning when they went to town to the sheriff's office.

And they took Pearl, and she told it was two of them. Mr. Jefferies also told them about Kate. But the sheriff said, "I don't have any proof that this happened."

Chapter 6

"**B**UT A WOMAN was beat up. I did not see this, and this—a white man, you say, that's killing your colored women—I will look into this."

Then Mr. Jefferies said, "I live on Mr. Colman's plantation in Drew, and he is trying to help me. The sheriff in Clarksville, he is also trying to help as well."

The sheriff said, "Okay, I will look into this, I promise you. Just go home, I will see you soon."

So they left and went home. Mr. Jefferies and his wife dropped off Pearl and Sam. Then they went back to Drew, the four of them, but this spread like wildfire.

The sheriff in Lealin called Mr. Colman and the mayor in Drew about this matter. When Mr. Jefferies, Marvin, and his wife got to Drew, Mr. Colman was sitting out in front of his house, waiting for Mr. Jefferies.

They pulled up, and Mr. Coleman said, "William,"—that was Mr. Jefferies' first name—"William, what's going on here? The sheriff called me from Lealin. Do you know what's happening on this lake?" Whore's Lake was on his land.

Just then, all four began to tell him, and all got into his car and drove down to the lake, trying to find out if this was really true. They looked and looked, then they found her clothing and whiskey in a bottle. The clothes were wet with piss and torn apart. When Mr. Colman saw her clothes and the whisky in the bottle, he cursed. "Why does he keep on doing this on my land, why?"

He got in his car and went to town. He told William, Marvin, and their wives to go home. "I got to figure this out myself. I can't take this anymore, just go home, William." Mr. Colman went and got his gun. His wife was trying to stop him but could not.

Mr. Colman went to the mayor's office in Drew. The mayor was worried because the sheriff from Lealin had called him and got him upset about Big John. Mr. Colman told the mayor, "I am tired of this man killing these colored women on my land. I have had enough."

The mayor said, "Please, Colman. Please, Colman, don't you do anything that you will be sorry for. I hate it too. John is messing up everything, he is a madman. What can we do? If we lock him up, he will get out soon. Then what can we do?"

Mr. Flemming said, "We all have to come to some kind of agreement." They tried to think of something. They did not want to kill him.

Mr. Colman said, "Let's all stay calm about this thing. Let's go and find him and talk to him." But Mr. Colman still had the gun, so they went in their cars to Big John's house—all three of them.

The door was closed, and the shades were drawn shut. It looked liked no one was there at that time, but his car was parked, plus fire and smoke were coming out of the chimney. They got out of their cars and went to the door and rang the bell. There was no answer; they rang it again. But again no one answered it. Then they knocked hard on the door and called him, "Big John, open the door." Then he came to open it.

He came to the door. Then he said, "What in the hell are you beating on my damn door like this for? What do you want?"

Mr. Colman said, "John, I want to know, were you on my land Thursday night?"

The mayor said, "Don't anyone get upset now. We just want to know John."

Then John said, "No. Who said I was on your land?" He went on to say, "I am so tired of all three of you, Colman." He added, "Mayor, I am sick of you all asking me, 'Did you kill that little black girl? Did you rape that nigger?'

"Yes, I killed them all. Now I told you I killed them all, I raped them all. Now what are you going to do to me, Mayor, for killing and raping a nigger? All you are crazy. We've been doing this for years, why are you so angry with me now, why?"

Mr. Colman pulled out his gun and shot John in the leg. The mayor fainted; he just stopped breathing, and they were screaming at each other. John ran through the house; blood was everywhere.

Mr. Colman ran to his car. Mr. Flemming was trying to get the mayor outside the door on the porch. John ran out back. People came outside to see what was going on, there was so much noise. John went to a doctor. The mayor went to a hospital there in town. Some of the neighbors helped Mr. Flemming with him because he was a heavy man. Mr. Colman went home; he wanted to kill John. He was so angry with John for what he was doing. This doctor treated all the people in the town, black and white.

When John got to the doctor, he was screaming about his leg. It was bleeding, and he was cursing Mr. Colman out. There was a young black man sitting there, waiting for the doctor. It was the Reverend James's son. John was the man who killed his two young sisters a while back.

This young man had so much anger for John in him because of what had happened to his sisters. And he felt that Big John got away because he was a white man.

Big John came in screaming, "Colman shot me!"

The doctor asked, "What happened to you, John? And cool down. I am not alone."

"I don't give a damn. He shot me about some nigger mess and their bodies on his land. Colman is a damn fool. That's what he is." This black boy was sitting and listening to him going on. "All our lives we been doing this for years, and now everybody's upset. And we been getting by too, you know it, Doc."

The doctor said, "John, please don't do this. I am not alone." John did not listen to him. James became so angry that he got up, picked up a stool, and hit Big John in the head and kept hitting him across the head. The doctor tried to stop him. "No, James, please don't do this." James did not stop until Big John was dead, then he ran home to his father, full of blood, crying, "Daddy, I killed Big John!"

His father was in the church praying when his son came in, covered of human blood.

His father began to cry. "Son, what you have done?"

His son, James Jr, said, "I just could not take anymore, Daddy. I would rather be dead." After that, he left running. James said on his way out the door, "Tell Mother bye for me, Daddy." His father just lay on the floor. "Oh no, my son! My son James!" The doctor ran for help from the office in the next room, screaming, "Help!" So the nurse and another doctor came in the room where John was murdered on the floor. There was blood everywhere so they called Mr. Colman and Mr. Flemming, and they all came to the clinic where they saw John lying in blood on the floor, dead. Mr. Flemming said, "What happened? Did Colman kill him?"

The doctor said, "No, James, the reverend's son did this to him."

Then Colman came in and looked. He asked, "What happened to him? Did you kill him, Flemming, for me?"

"No," Flemming said, "the son of Reverend James was here when John came to see the doctor after you shot him, Coleman, in the leg."

Chapter 7

THE DOCTOR SAID, "I could not stop John from talking about blacks and why he had been shot. Then James just went off. He started hitting John over the head with that stool until John was dead. He wanted him dead . . . all this blood on the floor."

Colman said, "I am glad John is dead. I hate that man. That black kid will probably die for a no-good white man."

Mr. Flemming said, "We got to go after this kid and bring him in. This is murder in Mississippi. You don't kill a white man. Not blacks." So they took John to the funeral home.

Then they got a couple of lawmen and went out to Rev. James's church and his house to ask him about his son. When they came to Rev. James's house, the whole family was out front, on the porch. Mr. Flemming asked Rev. James, "Where's your son? Is he in your house, Reverend?" Then Flemming went up on the porch and went through the house, looking for his son.

The reverend said, "My son was here but ran away. He just came to say good-bye."

Flemming started talking loudly, "Some of you know where he is, don't you? I should take all of you to jail for murder!"

The mother said, "I don't know. I didn't want Mr. John dead . . . and my son!" And she cried, "Oh Lord, help my son!"

Flemming said, "It's too late to cry, we need to find that boy soon."

Coleman said, "Leave these people alone, they had nothing to do with John's murder. Let's get the dogs and find him. Just leave them alone."

Flemming said to Rev. James and his family, "If anyone of you see him or if he comes back here, you better come and tell me in a hurry, you hear me? You all are in big trouble."

The James family said, "Yes, sir, we will."

Mr. Flemming got into his car and drove off. They were terrified of what had happened with James and Mr. John. No matter how this ended, James would be killed, and that was the painful part.

In the meantime, James Jr went into the woods. He did not stay on the road. He went to a neighbor's house and went into a side window and got his two guns.

Then James told his neighbor, "Tell my father and mother bye." Then he shot himself in the heart. The other plantation owner was screaming and was mad because they could not kill James Jr themselves. Mr. Colman said, "No, James, don't do it!" But it was too late; he was dead.

Then the other men ran down into the ditch and started beating James, calling him names, and got his body out of the ditch. They took James's body to town and laid him out on the street. They cut his ears off. Then beat him and kicked him after he was dead.

Mr. Colman went to James's family at midnight and told them everything that had happened. Then he said, "Leave now, every one of you, for your own good. I will help you if you don't have money to leave." So he gave them some funds and took some of them to the next town the next morning, and they left for Chicago. No one knew what they did with James's body.

This is the story of Whore's Lake.

www.ingramcontent.com/pod-product-compliance
Lightning Source LLC
Chambersburg PA
CBHW050349290526
45785CB00006B/2703